Every
Mother
Deserves a
Good Laugh

Every
Mother
Deserves a
Good Laugh

Julie Barnhill

Revell

a division of Baker Publishing Group
Grand Rapids, Michigan

© 2008 by Julie Barnhill

Published by Revell
a division of Baker Publishing Group
P.O. Box 6287, Grand Rapids, MI 49516-6287
www.revellbooks.com

Printed in the United States of America

ISBN 978-0-8007-1906-7

Published in association with the literary agencies of Alive Communications,
Inc., 7680 Goddard Street, Suite 200, Colorado Springs, Colorado 80920, and
Fedd & Company, Inc., 9759 Concord Pass, Brentwood, Tennessee 37027.

As women, we hold within our grasp
the power to change the world.

One family at a time.

One mother heart at a time.

We **don't** have to run for political office.
We **don't** have to write books.
We **don't** have to tell a hundred thousand
people the details of our journey.

No,

we can make all the difference

simply

by telling the truth of our life.

To ourselves first . . . then to **one another**.

Do you find yourself feeling

tire*d,*

weary,

worn out,

disappointed,

down,

discouraged,

stressed,

frustrated,

befuddled,

frazzled,

impatient,

taking yourself
a tad too seriously
for your own good,

tense,

bored,

uptight

- or just needing more (lots more!) laughter in your life?

Just between you and me—

each word of experience, prayer, insight, gentle warning, and real-life proof of lasting change mentioned within these pages was first tested and lived out (for better or worse) in my own family relationships as a mom.

You are not alone. Thousands upon thousands of women have shared with me personally via conversation, email, phone calls, or handwritten letters that, yes, even tough mothers struggle with the blues, stress, anger, and fleeting humor reserves.

The truth is, it isn't so much about getting everything right. Who among us reading these pages could honestly claim to have done that as a mother anyway? The important thing is acknowledging specific matters in our life as a mom for which we desperately need and desire change. And I can't think of anyone more willing and able to step up and do just that than me. So relax and stay a while as I dish up humorous advice and flat-out hilarious stories from the mothering trenches of life and children; they're sure to invoke a laugh or two and hopefully help you get your funny bone back.

A day
without
laughter

**is a day
wasted.**

Charlie Chaplin

It was a beautiful morning in 1990, and I was standing third in line with my eighteen-month-old daughter, Kristen, at our local bank. The lobby was bustling with customers, all waiting for overstressed tellers who would have preferred to be outside enjoying the weather rather than cashing endless checks.

The banking center had an open design (so "personal bankers" could see the comings and goings of customers), and glass walls afforded every titled management employee a front-row seat to any banking spectacles—such as the one I was about to present.

I can still remember distinctly the clothes Kristen and I were wearing that morning. Kristen sported a cute summer outfit with a large red strawberry embroidered on the shirt and tiny baby strawberries sprinkled across the fabric of her matching shorts. Her silky dark brown hair fell just to her shoulders and drew up into bouncy tendrils that framed her chocolate brown eyes.

Her smooth olive complexion and mischievous expression had caused more than one fellow mother/grandmother to exclaim, "She is simply adorable!"

I had delivered my second child, Ricky Neal, about three weeks before and was sporting the appropriate clothing for one who until recently had been very pregnant. My oversized T-shirt, knotted loosely at my hips (remember those fashion years?), strategically camouflaged the results of carrying a nine-pound-eight-ounce bundle of baby. The black, stretchy capri leggings, accented at the calves with a wide band of lace, did their best not to give away the Oreo cookie raids that had preceded his birth.

I wasn't as adorable as my toddler daughter that morning, but overall I felt pretty terrific. See, I had netted $717.83 from a garage sale the previous weekend. I got rid of nearly everything—a 4-H sewing machine, which confirmed my inability to match plaid fabric patterns; dining room furniture that had seen its best days about twenty years prior; and about anything else I could slap a price tag on. My home was less cluttered, and I stood in that bank lobby with my double-bagged plastic Wal-Mart sack weighted down with $717.83—mostly in quarters, dimes, nickels, and three pennies.

While Kristen and I waited, she entertained the captive audience with feats, such as spinning around until she was dizzy, scrunching her nose and lips to make an obnoxious breathing sound through her nostrils, and making faces at the people behind us. I, of course, was delighted to have such a cute and precocious child.

Sigh.

I had moved up to second in line when Kristen decided to turn her attention to me—her mother, the woman who had agonized fourteen hours— surviving on ice chips alone while her useless father ate McDonald's french fries right in front of me (not that I'm bitter)—to bring her into this world. Her mother, who thought the sun rose and set on her alone. Yes, she turned her attention to me—all eighteen mature months of it.

"Next," said the teller. I stepped to the window and plopped my double-bagged sack of dollars, quarters, nickels, dimes, and three pennies on the cool, marble countertop. Teller-girl threw me a wicked look and began sorting the coins.

"Oh!" I volunteered brightly, "I've already counted it and there is $717.83 . . . I got it all from a garage sale too!" I smiled. She cranked up the death-ray stare and continued.

Glancing back, I checked on Kristen and then rested my elbows on the countertop and daydreamed of all the things I could do with my windfall.

It was then I felt a small tentative poke to my, er, backside.

I ignored it. (Bad idea.)

Another small—but decidedly stronger than the first—poke against my backside, accompanied by the singsong voice of aforementioned adorable toddler proclaiming, "Big bottom, Momma! Big bottom!"

Poke, poke. Prod, prod.

I whipped around faster than you can say, "Go, Diego, go!" and saw my three-foot munchkin grinning from ear to ear. With each prod and poke, her tiny voice grew confident, bolstered no doubt by the smiles and chuckles of those in our immediate vicinity.

Lowering my head and unknotting my shirt, I whispered delicately, "Kristen, stop poking Mommy's bottom and quit saying 'big bottom.' It isn't nice to talk about Mommy's bottom and I don't want to hear you say that word again."

I turned back to the teller (who was trying to quell a smirk) and took pride in the fact that not a peep was being made behind me. That was a good thing, right? Uh, not so much. During the brief interlude Kristen was thinking, thinking, thinking—using the moments to formulate her strategy. And now the small poke flourished into an all-out punch.

With her tiny yet accurate fist she let loose one final punch and proclaimed for everyone (teller, personal banker, and middle management ensconced behind glass walls) to hear . . .

"Big butt, Momma! Big butt!"* (I did tell her not to say "bottom.")

---

*Adapted/excerpted from Julie Barnhill, *She's Gonna Blow: Real Help for Moms Dealing with Anger* (Eugene, OR: Harvest House, 2001), 17–20.

**Pretty much all the honest truth-telling
there is in the world is done by children.**

Oliver Wendell Holmes

On that beautiful spring day nearly twenty years ago, I had a decision to make—and fast! I could choose to melt into a puddle of humiliation, erupt just a tad in Mount Momma irritation, or simply laugh. I chose the latter, and I'd like to invite you to start doing more of the same.

Motherhood—The Job—is fraught with imperatives and matters of importance, both real and perceived. If allowed, we can easily become one seriously high-strung, uptight mother. Some of us already are! Admittedly, there are countless matters of grave importance when it comes to raising our children and taking care of parenting details, but this I know to be true also: we've got to lighten up and laugh, girls! The operative action phrase regarding this is as follows: we've got to *choose* to lighten up and laugh, girls!

Because you and I both know how it is as a mom.

We wake up with "Plans."

Important plans requiring detailed attention and serious consideration.

Time-restraint plans requiring on-time departures and arrivals.

Purchasing plans requiring the often painful involvement of toddlers and teens—acquiring new shoes, socks, lost binkies, non-lame jeans, T's (always the need for more of these!), project supplies, and a hundred and one other things.

You and I work our way through the day with certain unspoken goals:

Get through the day without eating nonstop.

Circumvent at least one potty-training accident.

Finish a full and complete thoug . . .

We're moms.

We have agendas and life-lesson plans.

We're moms.

And less and less often we make the choice to lighten up and laugh.

Enough of that, I say!

It's time our plans and goals included nurturing the serious business of humor in the realm of motherhood; tickling the funny bone and laughing so hard one snorts out loud. No one else can make it a priority but you. So for the next few minutes—for the next few pages—and then for the next few days and weeks of your life—choose to laugh.

Did You Know?

Babies first laugh around two to six months of age and do so by mimicking the behavior of parents and others around them.

Is there anything as infectious as a baby's laugh? (Okay, one exception: impetigo.)

Delighted moms and dads have posted innumerable videos online of their little one's raucous chortles and giggles. I have bookmarked one in particular, and when I find myself in need of a shot of comedic espresso, I simply click, listen, and have my mood lifted.

Laughing is a big deal in the Barnhill home, and I have delighted in watching my babies laugh out loud for the first time. I have even documented when it happened and what triggered it. (I don't do scrapbooks, but I'm a journal-writing fool!)

Kristen: November 25, 1988, three months old—
Daddy got you to laugh for the first time tonight.
You've smiled at him for a couple of weeks as he
made his faces and spoke silly to you. But tonight
you smiled, bonked him on the nose with your
little fist, and promptly gurgled and laughed with
glee. You have him wrapped around your little
finger, sweet girl.

Ricky Neal: July 27, 1990, exactly three months
old—Daddy said you laughed out loud while I
was out getting groceries. You are growing up so
fast.

Patrick: March 9, 1995, two months old—You
laughed out loud! Such a sweet chortle. You make
Mommy really work for her laugh (it took at least
six minutes of intense goofy faces and "puzzing"
you on the belly). But it's so worth it. Like the
peal of bells—JOYFUL!

I remember wondering, *How did they know to do
that, and where does this laughter spring from within
their little mind and soul?*

I'm not any closer to understanding the technicalities of it all than I was twenty years ago, but this I know: the trills and rollicking arpeggios of human laughter are surely audible proof of divine grace.

Children laugh an average of three to four hundred times a day.

Adults laugh only seventeen times.

And seventeen may well be pushing it for some.

Bear in mind also that when children laugh, they *really* laugh! If you've been unfortunate enough to be in a small enclosed space with multiple seven-year-old boys and then heard one of them poot (as in, expel gaseous fumes), well, trust me, no one is "tittering" with laughter or "chuckling" with glee. Nope. Those squirrelly XY chromosomes are letting loose with guttural glee.

And you? What's your average laugh level?

Do you prefer the "inside" laugh that one of my closest friends likes to remind me is just as much of a laugh as my somewhat loud and obnoxious guffaw?

Maybe you're like my husband and practice a more silent form of joviality. When Rick finds something or someone really, really, funny, he has this incredibly amusing way of scrunching his face, eyes kinda squinty, shoulders drawn up, and then silently laughing his head off. Watching him adds a minimum of five laughs to my daily score.

No matter the form, ladies, let me encourage you to increase your individual laughter statistics. Aim for nineteen laughs today. (Keep track!) Then add two more to that tomorrow. Let your laughter exponentially increase, and enjoy many of its benefits.

Laughter is a universal, inborn ability. Anyone can choose to laugh anytime, anywhere, and for no particular reason. The body doesn't know the difference between "real" laughter and simulated laughter, so you receive all the health and mood lifting benefits either way—so laugh already!

Studies show that laughter has a profoundly positive impact on both our physical and mental well-being.

Laughter . . .

reduces anxiety and stress,
oxygenates our blood and organs,
improves circulation, and releases
endorphins.

Laughter . . .

lifts our mood,
reduces blood pressure,
and strengthens our immune system.

Laughter . . .

increases learning and helps you (and your children) retain knowledge,

reduces pain,

and just feels good.

Laughter . . .

knows no cultural boundaries—you don't have to speak the same language to laugh with someone,

and nothing breaks the ice better when you're in a group situation—it is the one form of communication to which everyone can relate.

So why aren't more of us mothers laughing?

Well, it goes back to our plans and agendas and simply taking ourselves too seriously. I've seen it happen time and time again with countless women. They get pregnant, decide to adopt, have children, and little by little become overwhelmed by motherhood—The Job.

I swam in those waters a time or two, especially during the first year of our homeschooling experience. Aye, yi, yi! I was so intent on doing it "right" that I threw out levity completely. After all, I had been an elementary school teacher before becoming a mother, and I certainly didn't want to mess up my kids' education. (Who'd I have to blame but me?)

The result? Well, my kids could pass their math times test, differentiate long and short phonetic sounds, and identify the fifty states and their capitals—but rarely did we relax and intentionally add humor to our days. I sacrificed joy, relaxation, and the sheer delight of being a mom for the tyranny of "getting it right" and realized quickly enough it simply wasn't worth the cost.

After a much needed summer break, I approached our second and all subsequent school years with a decidedly different tone.

Laughter was going to be a core teaching and learning ingredient in the scope and sequence of my lesson plans. Simple things became important, such as allowing the children to do their schoolwork in our cozy living room, filled with the aroma of scented candles, rather than always "doing school" at the kitchen table; and purchasing and creating "fun sheets" for three-year-old Patrick to fill in and color so he could feel like a big kid too.

Nothing monumental, mind you, but each change was successful in contributing to a more restful, relaxing, and laughter-prone heart and home for my children and me.

I think we simply forget to laugh, as crazy as that sounds.

We grow up, get responsible, and find our minutes, hours, and days filled with thoughts about bills, breast versus bottle, potty training, pre-K, tumbling class, and a bazillion other adultlike mothering details.

We forget how to laugh.

We forget how good it feels to laugh.

Shoot! Some of us have even forgotten how to tell a great knock-knock joke!

My friends, these things ought not to be!

It's time for us to get serious about fun.

Hi, Lord,

It's me again—Serious Mother checking in.
I know I need to lighten up.
Laugh more.
Even learn a few jokes and goof around with the kids.
Yet I find it nearly impossible to do.
You know how it is—I mean, you see everything that goes on
around here anyway.
I start off with the best intentions.
"Be funny today," I tell myself.
Or at the very least, be less serious!
But then someone does something
(You know what I'm talking about!),
Or something unexpected messes with my day,
And I find myself back to square one.
Unfunny.
I'm going to need Your help with this, Lord.
Help me relax and see the humor in the "someones" and
"unexpected messes."
Help me lighten up and get out of Serious Mom mode.
Give me opportunities to laugh.
I mean, really laugh with my kids.
Even if it messes with my plans.

For Your Knock-Knock Pleasure

Memorize two or three of these old favorites and impress your children . . . and annoy your friends.

> Knock, knock.
> Who's there?
> Dewayne.
> Dewayne who?
> Dewayne the bathtub. I'm drowning!

> Knock, knock.
> Who's there?
> Doris.
> Doris who?
> Doris locked. That's why I had to knock!

> Knock, knock.
> Who's there?
> Normalee.
> Normalee who?
> Normalee I don't go knocking on doors,
>   but thanks for answering.

Knock, knock.
Who's there?
Keith.
Keith who?
Keith me and find out.

> Knock, knock.
> Who's there?
> I-8.
> I-8 who?
> I-8 lunch already. What's for supper?

Knock, knock.
Who's there?
Avenue.
Avenue who?
Avenue heard these knock-knock jokes
    before?

A
cheerful
HEART
is good medicine.

Proverbs 17:22

Out of the Mouths of
Other Mothers' Babes . . .

There's nothing like a true, well-told story to amp up the humor factor in our day. The following stories are a collection of tales that readers and event participants have sent me. Yes, they are all true, and each mom cheerfully signed permission to have hers printed for public consumption.

Do me a favor.

Read.

Laugh.

And then email me your personal favorite from your own family.

One afternoon I needed to use the restroom and my three-year-old daughter insisted on joining me. As I sat down on the seat, she looked at me solemnly, paused, sighed, and then shaking her head, said, "Oh, Mommy, you bottom is waaaaay too big for the potty."

Eileen D.

I invited some people to dinner. After everyone had found a seat around the table, I turned to my five-year-old daughter and asked, "Would you like to say the blessing?"

"I don't know what to say," she whispered.

"Just say what you've heard Mommy pray," I reassured her.

So she bowed her head, clasped her hands together, and said, "Dear Lord, why did I invite all these people to dinner?"

Rhonda W.

On the first day of school, a first-grader handed his teacher a note from his mother. The note read, "The opinions expressed by this child are not necessarily those of his parents."

Delana R.

A woman was trying hard to get the ketchup out of the jar. During her struggle the phone rang, so she asked her four-year-old daughter to answer the phone. "Mommy can't come to the phone to talk to you right now," the little girl said. "She's hitting the bottle."

Rory J.

While taking a routine vandalism report at an elementary school, I was interrupted by a little girl about six years old. Looking up and down at my uniform, she asked, "Are you a cop?"

"Yes," I answered and continued writing the report.

"My mother said, if I ever needed help, I should ask the police. Is that right?"

"Yes, that's right," I told her.

"Well, then," she said as she extended her foot toward me, "would you please tie my shoe?"

Natalie F.

A little boy opened the big family Bible. He was fascinated as he fingered through the old pages. Suddenly, something fell out of the Bible. He picked up the object and looked at it. It was an old leaf that had been pressed between the pages.

"Mama, look what I found," the boy called out.

"What have you got there, dear?"

With astonishment in the young boy's voice, he answered, "I think it's Adam's underwear!"

As told to Valerie W.

The youngest child of a close friend of mine was obsessed with anything and everything dealing with dinosaurs. Though only four years old, he devoured picture books and watched educational videos galore and could rattle off dinosaur facts like a madman.

One day, while he and his mother were shopping at the local Box-Mart, nature called, and off to the women's restroom they both went. Declaring himself, "big enough to do it by myself," he walked into an individual stall, closed and locked the door, and wiggled his way onto the seat.

My friend could see his sneakered feet dangling on the other side of the door. My friend and every other woman in the facility could hear his arduous efforts to cooperate with the call of nature.

On and on he went, increasing his dramatic vocalizing each passing moment. My friend thought she would pass out from embarrassment. Her son all but guaranteed it when he grunted and shouted, "Whoa! Watch out, Mom! I think I'm about to poop a T-Rex!"

Cynthia R.

Laughter is a celebration of our failings. That's what clowns are for. And that's what I am.

Emma Thompson

Laug

Laughter is part of the human survival kit.

David Nathan

Laughter is an instant vacation!

Milton Berle

hter

it is what it is . . .

Laughter is the jam on the toast of life. It adds flavor, keeps
it from being too dry, and makes it easier to swallow.

Diane Johnson

Clueless in Childbirth

Sometimes we're not laughing in the moment, but our experiences are storing up a treasure chest full of laughs for us to look back on. This is why I lead the bandwagon when it comes to writing down everything remotely funny or entertaining or amusing. Everything is fodder for a writer and even more so for moms. Check out my journal entry for August 17, 1988 (and yes, I really wrote it all as noted).

> 10:59 am—Dr. Wally just broke my water. It was pretty strange—he took what looked like a darning needle on steroids, smeared it and me with some Smucker's Grape Jelly looking stuff, and performed a half-stitch and wah-la! It didn't hurt at all, and I'm already dilated to 3cm and 50 percent effaced. Um, I have no idea what that means really but I'm sure it's a good thing. I have a feeling this first-born baby is going to get here fast.

11:20 am—Dr. Wally just left and told me to relax; it would probably be quite awhile until the baby arrives, he said. I don't think so. I know my body better than anyone and I have a feeling this is going to go fast.

12:10 pm—It's been awhile since Dr. Wally left. Rick is sitting here eating a Big Mac and fries and I was just told I can't have any real food until after delivery. I'm starving! Nobody told me about the food thing before this—I think I'm going to smack Rick.

1:45 pm—Mom and Dad just called. They are coming up with Grandma and I told them they better hurry. It's almost two hours from their home to the hospital. I'd hate for them to miss the delivery.

2:30 pm—I think I just had a contraction! Neat! I can't wait! I wish I could feel them more. Oh, yeah, Princess Fergie of England had a baby girl on the eighth of this month. This little one's arrival may not garner as much fanfare but I can't wait to hold him or her. Hurry up little one so I can see you!

4:18 pm—Mom and Dad are here. I'm able to smile through each contraction like nothing is happening. This isn't so bad. Mom is worried sick, and Grandma asked me if I had a girdle to put on after the baby arrives! She swears it'll keep my stomach flat. Hm? Interesting.

4:55 pm—Contractions are slightly stronger. I'm still smiling.

4:58 pm—Politely suggested (through clenched teeth) that Mom, Dad, and Grandma might want to go to dinner and come back a little later. (If I pressed my upper teeth into my bottom lip I could still smile while making said request.) Surely it can't be much longer . . . this is really beginning to hurt. Breathe, Julie, breathe . . . woo, woo, hee, woo, woo, hee.

5:08 pm—This hurts like a big dog! I am definitely and officially uncomfortable. I'm sitting in a Lazy-Boy (they need a Labor-Girl!) and I have on my house slippers that look like hound dogs. Just looking at them is starting to really annoy me. I don't recall anyone telling me about your entire rear-end going numb. I must be at least 6 or 7 cm by now.

6:12 pm—ONLY 4.5 cm??!! I quit.

7:32 pm—Good grief! Eight hours and no baby. I am not happy and I am not smiling. I would love some pain relief but Rick and I agreed beforehand that we'd do it natural. Rick's helping me breathe.

7:33 pm—Rick almost hyperventilated—someone get me a male nurse!

10:34 pm—I DEMAND AN EPIDURAL!

10:35 pm–12:45 am—Do I really want a ninety-seven-inch needle stuck in my back? Ugh. One minute I do. The next . . . not so much. They bring me Demerol instead and Julie is one happy contracting camper.

12:46 am—Happy camper has left the building! I cannot believe what just happened. I was in the middle of a horrific contraction, lying on my left side, rear end pointing towards the door, trying not to barf on anyone around me, when in walks Nurse #34 for the evening. I believe her last name was "Ratched."

"Julie," she barked, "I need to see how you're coming along, could you please get on your back for me?"

Who was she kidding? Get on my back? Get on my back!

I shifted the three pillows from between my legs; asked Rick to move the pillow pressed behind my back, and then pathetically flopped my comatose tush and legs until I was . . . sigh . . . on my back.

"Happy?!"

Applying more Smuckers (insert "Jaws" musical theme) she approached as a gargantuan contraction hit and I closed my eyes (big mistake!) . . . Aieeeeeeeeee! Nobody ever told me about that! I am ready to crack some heads.

12:47–3:02 am—Unable to effectively communicate without unseemly gestures.

3:03 am—"Julie, you can push now!"

3:52 am—It's a girl! Welcome Kristen Jean Barnhill . . . I knew you'd get here fast.

There is a time for everything . . .
a time to weep and a time to laugh.

Ecclesiastes 3:1, 4

I'd just finished preparing a yummy breakfast for my three-year-old son, Patrick, and was walking back toward the kitchen sink when he asked, "Hey, Momma, why's your bottom do this [jiggling motion with both hands] when you walk?"

My second favorite household chore is ironing.
My first being hitting my head on the top bunk bed until I faint.

Erma Bombeck

My mother taught me to read when I was three years old (her first mistake). One day I was in the bathroom and noticed one of the cabinet doors was ajar. I read the box in the cabinet. Then I asked my mother why she was keeping napkins in the bathroom. Didn't they belong in the kitchen? Not wanting to burden me with unnecessary facts, she told me that those were for special occasions.

Now fast forward a few months. It's Thanksgiving Day, and my folks are leaving to pick up the pastor and his wife for dinner. Mom had assignments for all of us while they were gone. Mine was to set the table. You guessed it!

When they returned, the pastor came in first and immediately burst into laughter. Next came his wife, who gasped and then began giggling. Next came my father, who roared with laughter. Then came Mom, who almost died of embarrassment when she saw each place setting on the table with a "special occasion" napkin at each plate, with the fork carefully arranged on top. I had even tucked the little tails in so they didn't hang off the edge. My mother asked me why I used these and, of course, my response sent the other adults into further fits of laughter. "But, Mom, you *said* they were for special occasions!"

Author unknown

Authors and speakers who'll help you flex your funny muscles . . .

Erma Bombeck

The Grand Dame of comedic writing, Erma knew and practiced the Golden Rule of column writing: "Hook 'em with the lead. Hold 'em with laughter. Exit with a quip they won't forget." Her observations withstand the test of time and no one is her equal. Grab as many of her books as you can. Read them. Quote them. And perhaps attend the Erma Bombeck Humor Writer's Workshop and discover your own talents just lying beneath the surface. Here are some of Erma's books you shouldn't miss:

The Grass Is Always Greener over the Septic Tank

If Life Is a Bowl of Cherries, What Am I Doing in the Pits?

When God Created Mothers

A Marriage Made in Heaven: Or Too Tired for an Affair

The Best of Bombeck: At Wit's End, Just Wait until You Have Children, I Lost Everything in the Post-Natal Depression

Cathy Guisewite

Cathy has entertained readers for more than twenty-five years, starting with her syndicated comic series, *Cathy*, which, by the way, was launched after her mother urged her to submit her doodles to Universal Syndicate Press. See, moms, it pays to know funny. One of my personal book favorites written and illustrated by Cathy is *Mom: A Celebration of One of Four Basic Guilt Groups.* The remaining three guilt groups are food, work, and love. Here are some others to enjoy:

Motherly Advice from Cathy's Mom

Confessions to My Mother

Abs of Steel, Buns of Cinnamon: A Cathy Collection

How to Get Rich, Fall in Love, Lose Weight, and Solve All Your Problems by Saying "No": A Cathy Coping Guide for the '80s (I love it, just for all the cultural reminders of my era.)

Anita Renfroe

I first met Anita at a speakers' brunch in 2001. She wasn't actually sitting in her seat but had left her eyeglasses—her highly decorated and unique eyeglasses—lying on her placemat. One glance at those babies and I thought to myself, *Now this is a woman I could be friends with!*

Indeed, I could.

Fast forward a few years and you'll find she's still sporting übercool frames and a comedy-parody talent unlike anyone you've probably ever met. Her clips online have launched her into another stratosphere of motherhood and comedy. Here are some of Anita's books:

If It's Not One Thing, It's Your Mother

If You Can't Lose It, Decorate It: And Other Hip Alternatives to Dealing with Reality

Jenn Doucette

Jenn is an up-and-coming comedy writer and performer, and you're going to be glad I told you about her. I swear she's Jim Carrey's twin, what with her elasticized expressions and gravity-defying eyebrows. "G-rated giggles and good clean fun" is her motto, and her books and speaking prove it time and time again.

Check out her stand-up speaking topics and consider booking her for your next comedy event:

Tales from the Crib
Laughter Therapy
Last Mom Standing

And her books:

Mama Said There'd Be Days Like These
Velveteen Mommy

Lysa TerKeurst

My friend Lysa is funny—laugh-out-loud funny. She can spin a yarn better than anyone else I know. But what I love the most about Lysa is that she knows how to make you think much deeper than you ever thought possible. She knows the true power of humor: it demystifies the speaker and writer and reveals a real woman and mother desperate for an authentic life of faith. Read her books and laugh your way to a deeper place of faith.

The Bathtub Is Overflowing, but I Feel Drained
What Happens When Women Say Yes to God?
What Happens When Women Walk by Faith?
Who Holds the Keys to Your Heart?

Funny Movies for Your Consideration

The following selections are from my own personal favorites growing up, as well as movies I've watched with my children.

The Princess Bride. This movie offers some of the all-time best quotes that you can adopt as your own! Over time, our family has created a *Princess Bride* language understood by us alone. And that, my friends, is one of the best things you can do as a mom—create your own humor haven of connectedness.

Airplane! I'm dating myself, but I still love the blustering goofball parody of this movie.

A Fish Called Wanda. One of Kevin Kline's best-ever roles.

This Is Spinal Tap. I'm a huge fan of Christopher Guest, but his stuff is high on the quirky scale— just so you know. People tend to love his stuff or they repeat over and over, "I just don't get it." There are three people in my movie-viewing universe who will sit with me through this movie and laugh until our sides hurt. As such, material is geared more for moms and should be enjoyed with like-quirky-minded friends and adults.

It's a Mad, Mad, Mad, Mad World (original 1963). I watched this once a year with my mom and dad as a young grade-schooler. Even then I was drawn to over-the-top fun!

What About Bob? You'll want to be sure to check out this comedy and banter about one of its most famous lines, "I'm sailing! I'm sailing!"

A Christmas Story. This was a bit more fun before TNT ran it in back-to-back marathons. Nevertheless, Ralphie never ceases to make us laugh.

Laugh and the world
laughs with you. Weep
and you weep alone.

Ella Wheeler Wilcox

Laughter and Girlfriends

Ah, the memories—cruising in a sporty car, radio blasting with Bryan Adams wailing away, and laughing my head off as my best friends in high school, Cindy and Shelly, tried to get the attention of the male driver of a Ford pickup truck behind us.

I missed those days, so one summer evening in 2002, around age thirty-five or so, I piled my adult girlfriends Margie, Kate, and Toni into my sporty 1990 Chevy Lumina APV and took them on an adventure to remember. Just a few months before, I had told CPA friend Margie she needed to lighten up a bit and let go of some of her tax-time angst. She wasn't so sure. But once I convinced Kate (my girlfriend who laughed at everything) and Toni (my girlfriend who had the gift of egging me on in times of crisis or prime entertainment potential), I knew she couldn't resist.

At the time, about the only thing that worked on the vehicle was the ignition key. A rubber bumper strip had fallen off and had left a lovely glue streak down the entire right side. The passenger door had to be opened from the inside, and the interior dome lights did not work.

And should I feel the need to load a cart full of groceries through the rear hatch, it would first require my climbing over the second- and third-row seats and popping it open from the inside.

That was the vehicle my girlfriends piled into—with little complaint. Then we proceeded to crank up the radio—listening to the classic rock sounds of Journey (*note*: I was supposed to marry Steve Perry; he didn't get the memo)—and cruised around the city of Galesburg, Illinois.

Yes, I said "cruised."

Downtown we went, pulling up next to a souped-up piece of vehicular art. I looked at the eleven-year-old driver, revved my six-cylinder engine, and visually challenged him to a runoff.

He looked at me like I was an idiot.

It empowered me all the more.

"Hey, little guy!" I shouted after lowering my electronic window by pushing on the control button and forcing the glass down with my other hand, "Do you wanna go or not?" *Varoom . . . varoom . . .*

Again the stare.

My girlfriends were dying—from embarrassment and laughter.

Then I peeled out—well, better stated, I put the accelerator to the floorboard and sorta chugged my way six or seven feet in twenty seconds and ambled over to the bank parking lot where all hormonally driven teens are required by law to meet and hang out.

Pulling into the drive, I leaned my head out the window again and shouted to no one in particular, "Hey, your momma called and said it was time for you to come home."

Then I laughed so hard and sang so loud over the next two hours (we were all home in bed by 10:53 p.m.) that I lost my voice for the following day or two.*

That, my friend, is an evening well spent!

---

*Adapted/excerpted from Julie Barnhill, *Scandalous Grace* (Carol Stream, IL: Tyndale, 2004), 115–16.

Sage Advice from a Barnhill Underling

Make sure you swallow your drink
before you start laughing hard.
It really hurts when soda
shoots out your nose. But it's way cool!

Patrick Barnhill

A Picture of What's to Come?

Several years ago, I found myself at the Hartsfield-Jackson International Airport in Atlanta, Georgia, with a four-hour, unscheduled layover.

I had managed to entertain myself for an hour with a Philly cheesesteak sandwich, as well as a scoop of Ben & Jerry's mint chocolate chunk ice cream. But with three hours remaining, I proceeded to haul my faux-leather carry-on (roughly the size of a small microwave) through the WHSmith bookstore.

Maybe it was the size of my bag or the eight hard-back books I managed to knock from their display, but I got the distinct impression (security following behind me, speaking in hushed tones) that store management would prefer I move on.

I can take a hint, and I needed to visit the ladies' restroom anyway.

As I walked toward the entrance, two older women came in behind me. Laughing comfortably with each other, they began to "talk shop":

Grandchildren.
Retirement funds.
Bunion surgery.
Plans for the holidays.
You name it; they dished about it.

I waited for an available stall, and they made their way to the heavily lit, mirrored vanity across from the stalls spanning the length of the room.

I had just stepped into a stall and locked the door when I overheard one of them say, "Honestly, Helen, would you just take a look at my stomach in these pants."

Voyeuristically peeking through the gap between stall wall and door, I leaned forward and observed Stomach Girl and her girlfriend Helen.

Stomach Girl continued, "I mean, really, it looks just awful in these pants." She then began to pat herself down as we women are wont to do when it comes to bulging areas on our body. She turned this way and that way. Sucked in her stomach muscles— let her stomach muscles out. Pulled her shirt out of her waistband and knotted it. Tucked her shirt back into her waistband and sighed.

Back and forth she went, on and on, gazing at her reflection in the mirror, until, finally, Helen could stand it no longer. Looking directly into the eyes of her seemingly dear friend, she admonished, "Oh, please, June. You look perfectly fine in those pants. Your stomach looks fine in those pants. I don't know what you're complaining about, anyway . . ."

Pregnant pause.

"If you really want to see an awful stomach, take a look at mine."

(I know, I know . . . I should have flushed and looked away. But I'm telling you, it was like passing a train wreck . . . you know it's going to be ugly but you . . . just . . . can't . . . avert . . . your . . . gaze.)

And then, to my voyeuristic horror, Helen pulled down her waistband and Hanes and let us all take a gander!

June looked at Helen.

Helen looked at June.

And I nearly passed out. (Trust me, it's hard to argue with a 1960s-era gallbladder scar and puddles of loose flesh.)

Then, without skipping a beat, June said, "You're right, your stomach looks *much* worse than mine."

Helen smiled, snapped her pants back into place, and then roaring with laughter made her way arm-in-arm with June toward the concourse.*

I have seen the future . . . and it makes me smile.

---

*Excerpted from Barnhill, *Scandalous Grace*, 29–31.

Girlfriend . . .

You were born a daughter.
you looked up to your mother.
you looked up to your father.
you looked up to everyone.
you wanted to be a princess.
you wanted to own a horse.
you wanted your brother to be a horse.

you wanted to wear pink.
you never wanted to wear pink.
you wanted to be a veterinarian.
you wanted to be president.
you wanted to be the president's
        veterinarian.

you were picked last for the team.
you were the best one on the team.
you refused to be on the team.

you wanted to do well in algebra.
you hid during algebra.

you wanted boys to notice you.
you were afraid the boys would notice you.
you started to get acne.
you started to get breasts.
you started to get acne that was bigger than
    your breasts.

you wouldn't wear a bra.
you couldn't wait to wear a bra.
you couldn't fit into a bra.

you didn't like the way you looked.
you didn't like the way your parents looked.
you didn't want to grow up.

you had your first best friend.
you had your first date.
you spent hours on the telephone.

you got kissed.
you got to kiss back.
you went to the prom.
you didn't go to the prom.
you went to the prom with the wrong
    person.

you spent hours on the telephone.
you fell in love.
  you fell in love.
    you fell in love.
you lost your best friend.
you lost your other best friend.
        you *really* fell in love.

you became a steady girlfriend.

Sooner or later, you start to take yourself
  seriously.
you know when you need a break.
you know when you need a rest.
you know what to get worked up about,
and what to get rid of.

you know when it's time to take care of
  yourself,
to do something for yourself that makes you
  stronger, faster, more complete because
  you know it's never too late to live life
  and never too late to change one.

Laughter and Real Life . . .

As I noted previously, all of life is fodder when it comes to adding laughter to our days. It comes back again to the matter of choice—choosing to find and see and acknowledge the humor of a situation, choosing to adjust your ears and eyes to the "quirk factor" of any given moment and giving in to it. The following excerpts do just that—highlighting the obscure, the ridiculous, and XX-chromosome-related realities, as well as acknowledging the weariness even a well-tended humorous mother soul can feel.

Wanted for Attempted Murder
(the actual AP headline)

Linda Burnett, 23, was visiting her in-laws, and while there went to a nearby supermarket to pick up some groceries. Several people noticed her sitting in her car with the windows rolled up and with her eyes closed, with both hands behind her head.

One customer who had been at the store awhile became concerned after an hour, and walked over to the car. He noticed that Linda's eyes were now open, and she looked very strange. He asked her if she was okay, and Linda replied that she'd been shot in the back of the head and had been holding her brains in for over an hour.

The man called the paramedics, who broke into the car because the doors were locked and Linda refused to remove her hands from her head. When they finally got in, they found that Linda had a wad of bread dough on the back of her head.

A Pillsbury biscuit canister had exploded from the heat, making a loud noise that sounded like a gunshot, and the wad of dough hit her in the back of her head. When she reached back to find out what it was, she felt the dough and thought it was her brains. She initially passed out but quickly recovered and tried to hold her brains in for over an hour until someone noticed and came to her aid.*

---

*Okay, full disclosure here: this is one of those "hard-to-nail-down-as-jello" stories that periodically pops up as complete truth or utter fabrication both online and through word of joke-telling mouth. As such, I shall simply present it to you, dear mothers, as a tale too ticklish not to tell. You decide on the veracity.

Best-Laid Plans

I had everything prepared.

My mandatory tablet of unused, yellow legal paper and "everyone keep their hands off!" favorite writing pen. Bibles and various resource tools were piled high on my desk. I was ready to get to work.

Then it happened.

Rather, "he" happened.

My youngest, Patrick Michael, chose at that precise moment to act incredibly and shamefully cute. I attempted to ply him with binky and sippy cup in his playpen.

Patrick would have nothing to do with such nonsense.

He was outraged, I tell you!—well, in a thoroughly sixteen-month-old manner. He decided to unleash a round of artillery against me—a cherubic smile and arms outreached while grunting, "Eh, eh, eh, eh, eh."

Determined to work, I proceeded with plan A.

Patrick resorted to plan B—lying on his blanket, he pulled his chubby toes toward his mouth, while cooing and gurgling adorably.

Ugh. I had been dealt a mortal blow.

Shards of emotional shrapnel eviscerated my work plans as I succumbed to his charms, bent down, and seized a giggling mass of baby.

He had won—and knew it. Reveling in my defeat, a smile flitted across his round face as if to say, "Sucker!"

Some Days Laughter Doesn't Come So Easy . . .

My day begins. So simply stated one could easily misconstrue it as a mere blip on the screen of life, the seemingly insignificant task of yawning, stretching, and appealing to the alarm clock for one more minute for a weary mother.

I extricate myself from cozy, heated bed coverings, willing myself against the slap of coldness that awaits both feet and soul. It is at this moment I feel most vulnerable.

Far from awaking refreshed, I find myself fighting the residue of an evening spent "catching up." All reasons for staying awake until 2:00 am now escape me and seem foolish. Slothfully, I make my way to the kitchen, anticipating the solace of a steaming cup of toffee-flavored hot chocolate.

The flesh is now warm but the spirit listless. I must also find an antidote for the cheerlessness of my heart. Soon children will charge down the steps, demanding, questioning, and looking to their mom as an anchor in the midst of morning chaos.

"Lord, allow the love of Your Spirit to renew my heart and spirit. I am weary and so very tired and have zero get-up-and-go strength of my own."

Then, as sure as the sunrise, He makes Himself known to me.

Again I am humbled to think that the God of all the universe would care for me here in this quiet and lonely hour.

No lightning bolts. No scrolls across the sky.

It is in the stillness, the quietness of the morning, that I hear Him gently command, "Seize the day and lighten up already!"

My feet are still cold.

And I hear the rustling of bedcovers and count the seconds until three eager faces appear, transforming my day of mere existence to eternal significance.

I refuse to think of them as chin hairs. I think of them as stray eyebrows.

Janette Barber

Laughter and Aging

I was teaching a unit on Florida to my fourth graders prior to a field trip to St. Augustine, showing a book with pictures of the building of the railroad by Flagler. One of my students asked me: "Were the streets black and white back then?" After recovering my jaw from the floor, I asked her to please tell me she was kidding. She wasn't.

Ada

An Older Mother's Revenge

When I'm a little old lady
Then I'll live with my children
and bring them great joy.
To repay all I've had
from each girl and boy

I shall draw on the walls
and scuff up the floor;
Run in and out
without closing the door.

I'll hide frogs in the pantry,
socks under my bed.
Whenever they scold me,
I'll hang my head.

I'll run and I'll romp,
always fritter away
The time to be spent
doing chores every day.

I'll pester my children
when they are on the phone.
As long as they're busy
I won't leave them alone.

Hide candy in closets,
rocks in a drawer,
And never pick up my clothes
off from the floor.

Dash off to the movies
and not wash a dish.
I'll plead for allowance
whenever I wish.

I'll stuff up the plumbing
and deluge the floor.
As soon as they've mopped it,
I'll flood it some more.

When they correct me,
I'll lie down and cry,
Kicking and screaming,
not a tear in my eye.

I'll take all their pencils
and flashlights, and then
When they buy new ones,
I'll take them again.

I'll spill glasses of milk
to complete every meal,
Eat my banana and
just drop the peel.

Put toys on the table,
spill jam on the floor,
I'll break lots of dishes
as though I were four.

What fun I shall have,
what joy it will be
To live with my children . . .
the way they lived with me!

Author unknown

Mirth is God's medicine.
Everybody ought
to bathe in it.

Henry Ward Beecher

Perhaps the cover of this book caught your eye on a Store-Mart shelf, grocery store kiosk, or library display. Maybe a mothers' group or book club you participate in chose it as their monthly pick, or you found it lying beneath a pile of stacked reference materials in your physician's waiting room. Perhaps someone purchased it *for* you and/or recommended it *to* you, and, given the title, you're just not quite sure what to think. Or perhaps you simply picked it up because it aptly describes where you have been or the place in which you currently find yourself as a mom.

No matter the path that brought you here, I'm so glad you came.

I tried my best to set out a quick-to-read layout, easy to digest and easy to go to as a reference point in time(s) of need. I included all sorts of quotable quotes that you can tuck away in your memory and use as encouragement for yourself and others, as well as truth found in the Bible.

You see, this one thing I know to be true: change—true and lasting change for our weaknesses, failings, weariness, and worries—can and will ultimately come as the result of truth penetrating our hearts.

I know from raw personal experience that it is impossible to change oneself by self-will alone—at least any lasting change. Oh, we can vow to "do better" and all that jazz but eventually, well, eventually we find ourselves back to square one because we're altogether human and finite and limited.

But the truth of Scripture penetrating our heart brings about an entirely different result. When we hear and accept the truth of God's Word and open our eyes to the divine appropriateness of laughter in our lives as mothers, it changes our heart—the core of who we are, how we feel, how we act, and what we believe. When our heart changes, our thoughts change. And when our thoughts change, our actions change. And when our thoughts and our actions change, our words and feelings change. And it is then, my sweet friend, when you see lasting change in yourself and in your family.

So if you rushed through or ignored those important words that I quoted from other people or from the Bible, I want to encourage you to go back and reread their wisdom. You may even want to grab a few of those infamous Post-its and mark two or three of your favorites.

Read through them and ask God to show you one in particular that may give you comfort, grace, teaching, and change. Copy it and post it near the places you frequent: kitchen, bathroom, baby's changing station, and minivan. Post it, read it aloud, believe it, and live for yourself the truth it contains.

I hope my own confessions of shared struggles and countless discoveries of hope and change along the way have helped you feel less alone. I am more convinced each year I live, write, and speak with women that hearing and reading the unvarnished truth of someone else's story is paramount in our belief that we are not the only ones battling and struggling.

And last but not least, I hope the personalized prayers touched your mothering heart and spirit. I get to do a lot of amazing things and have traveled across the world—literally—but time and time again this consistency remains: I find praying for individuals, one-on-one, undoubtedly to be my favorite thing to do. As you pray, I'd like you to imagine me standing with you—in front of you with my left hand placed on your right shoulder and my right gently pressed against the back of your neck. Our heads are bowed— foreheads leaning toward one another—as we simply talk real with God about our needs and His ability to meet them.

That's all.

No fill-in-the-blanks.

No tests or teaching points to ponder.

It's just you and me touching base in the most meaningful and relaxed manner I know how. So enjoy, my friend, and know I'm cheering for you from across the miles, cheering and praying peace, joy, contentment, and confidence into your life as a woman and mom. I'll look forward to hearing from you personally as a result of our time together.

Until then!

Julie

Julie Barnhill
julie@juliebarnhill.com
onetoughmothertalk.blogspot.com

More Mothering Resources

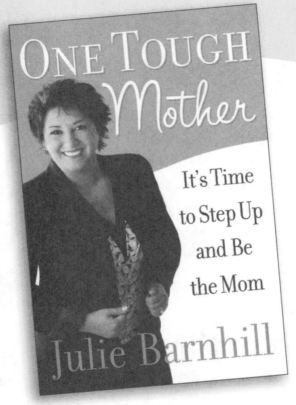

ONE TOUGH Mother

It's Time to Step Up and Be the Mom

Julie Barnhill

Visit Julie's blog at
www.onetoughmotherbook.com

from Author
Julie Barnhill

Better together...

**MOPS is here to come alongside you
during this season of early mothering to
give you the support and resources you
need to be a great mom.**

Get connected today!

Mothers of Preschoolers

2370 S. Trenton Way, Denver CO 80231
888.910.MOPS • **www.MOPS.org/bettermoms**